ADVANCED

CRYPTOCURRENCY

A definitive guide to advanced levels of trading with crypto coins

By **George Samaris**

Table of Contents

Introduction

If you know what cryptocurrency is about, you will agree that it is an ever-evolving concept with different parts, ideas and notions. There are no unique approaches to considering cryptocurrencies because as the year goes by, novel tools and inventions are created by developers and crypto coin enthusiasts.

This book is a continuation of a series of thoughts I have shared with you in previous editions; we started by building on the concept of cryptocurrency for beginners, then moved on to an intermediate phase and now are at the advanced stage.

An advanced level with anything means a more sophisticated approach as such we will be considering higher aspects of cryptocurrencies that give you a glimpse into what the future holds for digital coins.

Regardless of how vested you are with cryptocurrencies (as an investor, buyer or seller), you must be interested in what happens in the industry. The chapters below are replete with information on some of the recent trends, tools, ideas and concepts that have shaped the crypto world in recent times.

You will discover some old ideas you are familiar with and then also unravel some new ideas. In the end, you will be updated on all things crypto and this knowledge will help you make better decisions as you invest in the coming years.

The only thing required of you while reading is to implement everything you discover (this is so important). Success is a combination of KNOWLEDGE + ACTION; first, you get to know something and then you need to apply what you know else the knowledge will go to waste. Make up your mind today to get the BEST out of this book, and you will be amazed at the level of progress you make.

A lot of information you read through may be strange at first, but you can rest easy knowing that they will be demystified. Do your best to bring the words you read here to live; as you read seek out areas in your life and crypto investing where you can implement the knowledge you've gained.

Alright, we have had enough of the introductory talks, it is time to get started, and our first point of call is an analysis of the circles of cryptocurrencies. We will consider the then, now and future; it promises to be exciting one so head over there and read through now.

CHAPTER ONE

Cryptocurrency; Before, Now and Future

Cryptocurrency is an ever-evolving concept; what you know about it long ago is entirely different from what you will discover in this book. If you are interested in cryptocurrencies, then you must be proactive with seeking knowledge and information. In this chapter, we try to strike a balance between the different experiences we've had with cryptocurrencies in the past, what is obtainable now and what we can expect in the future.

At the end of this chapter, you will be able to grasp an understanding of what we have gained from cryptocurrencies, what we are still working with and what to expect in the future.

Cryptocurrency then

Cryptocurrency in the past was a novel venture so many people didn't understand. It started to increase in popularity when investors began to see the positive impact it had on the finances of those who tried it cryptocurrencies had a significant boost.

Due to the initial uncertainties that plagued the currencies, there were fewer coins, Bitcoin reigned supreme at the time, and it was the only viable option investors had. Cryptocurrency then was all about trial by error because they were fewer books that explained basic concepts and people just tried to do what they thought was best.

So, at these initial times, other people learnt from the mistakes of investors, oh, and there were a lot of errors. Summarily, cryptocurrencies were not at the very top then regarding financial considerations; only a few dared to invest, and only a few saw the potential it had in the future.

Cryptocurrency now

Today, cryptocurrencies are in bloom. Oh, there is a world of difference between what was obtainable in the past and what we enjoy now. There is even greater liberty to explore with digital coins, and it is all because of the myriad of options available on the scene.

There are more cryptocurrencies in the market today and unlike in the past more open are open about investing and doing it the right way. More importantly, the technology that backs up cryptocurrencies has improved thus making room for new inventions that are strategic in shaping the user experience.

There are over 1,000 crypto coins currently; Bitcoin, though a leading currency isn't the only option we have, and this has given a market a significant boost. Today there are vital concepts such as Airdrops, ICOs, STOs etc. that add a lot of value to the crypto experience.

More so, crypto coins can be used for various services today than in the past. Now we can buy items online and offline paying with crypto coins. We can get gifts for those we love with cryptos, and we can do a whole lot of other things with cryptocurrencies.

What we had in the past laid the foundation for what we are enjoying today. All of the issues, stiff regulations and problems cryptocurrencies faced in the past prepared it for world dominance in the present. Presently, cryptocurrencies are still met with the same level of volatility it had in the past so despite the progress there are still issues that must be dealt with in the future.

Cryptocurrency in the future

We can get a glimpse into the future from what we have seen in the past and present. Experts have predicted that because of the lack of regulation and centralised authority with cryptocurrencies it will still be volatile.

It is also predicted that there will more coins, but if they are unable to seize their position in the market, they will become vulnerable enough to lose their value. More countries will most likely adopt the concept of a decentralised currency, and this will make it easier for a lot of people to become vested in cryptocurrencies.

In the future, there will be more retails outfits that accept crypto coins. Presently it is so easy to make payments with tokens, and if it continues, there will be an increase in awareness on how people can make payment with ease using digital coins. When there are more acceptance centres, more value will be placed on cryptocurrencies.

In the future, it is postulated that more countries might not want to make cryptocurrencies legal because they wouldn't want it to replace their national currency. There will also be an increase in digital apps that make it possible for cryptos to be used efficiently and this will contribute immensely in making the investment process seamless.

There is so much to look forward in the future, while we wait for it to be unravelled before us we must utilise all we have today and make the best use of cryptocurrencies, so the future is guaranteed.

When you decide to invest in a venture, the first step you should take is to ascertain if the platform suits your plans for the investment. So many people invest in cryptos because everyone else is doing it and this is a very wrong approach. The fact that everyone is doing something doesn't mean you are prepared for it.

You must look through the past, try to understand it and then consider the future from the present perspective. After evaluation, you will be able to get a clear perspective on the investment opportunity and make the best choices. With cryptocurrencies extra caution must be applied; the market is quite unpredictable so be prepared for anything.

This chapter is just a foundation on which every other idea we learn in later chapters will be implemented. We will begin the journey properly with the section that covers the concept of blockchain evaluation; do enjoy the read.

CHAPTER TWO

The Need For Blockchain Evaluation

The blockchain is one of the most crucial aspects of cryptocurrency; it is impossible to speak about cryptocurrencies and not put blockchain in perspective because that is the platform where every transaction is recorded and made public.

In this chapter, we will be evaluating the blockchain because we are on a mission to understanding advanced cryptocurrency so that we will consider the technical viability of the platform and other factors.

The blockchain has the potential to provide solutions to the problem's businesses are faced with especially in cases where the processes can be streamlined across organisations that help parties transacts effectively. There are a lot of business scenarios that make it look like if blockchain is involved, the process will be better, but until there is the proper evaluation, such situations cannot be considered.

Two areas concerning blockchains must be considered; its viability and its suitability.

Viability with business

For you to determine the business suitability you must consider three factors that are in the form of questions;

1. Do the companies in various companies share the data in the business process?
2. Is verification of data and transactions between business partners required?
3. Must the parties read and update the data?
4. Should asset transfers between parties check?

When these answers are considered, one can go right ahead with the business plan, but if the answers are majorly answered in the negative, then blockchain may not be the right fit for the business. If the answers are mostly in the positive, then you must take steps to discover the requirements needed to plan and assess critical areas.

After getting a full assessment of the situation, you will have to choose between building a system or getting integrated into one. You must decide if your company will found a blockchain solution or become a member of the more extensive blockchain network. If you are going to build, how do you make sure it is built to the right specification?

A lot of organisations and companies are evaluating blockchains for the benefits of exploring the optimisation of processes and saving cost. They also seek to create services that will generate new revenue streams. A lot of large companies are engaged in blockchain because they know that the increasing growth of these collaborations will advance the standards of their enterprise and maximise the shared benefits from blockchain solutions.

Technical Viability

After going through the processes above, you will need to consider the technical aspects of the process. First, you should ensure that the solutions fit with your blockchain platforms and it has the capabilities you require. Please note that the technology changes with time, so it is essential that your business evolves with it.

There are some technical questions you should ask before going ahead to utilise blockchain for your business., you will find them below;

1. What is the consensus protocol that suits the solution?
2. What are the transaction and contract privacy needed for the answers?
3. Do you require a specific governance model for changes with the blockchain network?

The answers to the questions above will determine the areas of customisation or extension that may be required to achieve the kind of capabilities you seek technically. When you establish technical viability, you can start designing solutions that are flexible so they can remain in use even when the technology evolves.

Changes with blockchain often have to do with approaches that start with the augmentation of business processes and then it builds on decentralised models.

Return on investment could be incremental as the solution continually evolves; so you would have to build a strategy with the apparent scope as it is key to discovering the sustainability of the blockchain, understand the Return of investment and gain access to technical viability.

With blockchain evaluation, you can be sure of gaining insight into how blockchain will become profitable for your business or not. There are no other short-cuts to ensuring that this is the path to take; you've got to evaluate whatever process you will be utilising on your business before the implementation phase.

A very critical aspect of cryptocurrency that must be considered is the idea of hard and soft forks; we are going to discuss how these ideas affect your investment process, head over there now and read on.

GEORGE SAMARIS

CHAPTER THREE

The Concept of Hard and Soft forks

So what are forks? And what connection do they have with cryptocurrencies?

A fork is a programming term that refers to an open-source code modification. Most times the forked code is like the original but with some crucial adjustments. A fork can be used to test a process, but only with cryptocurrencies, it is also used to implement changes or create a new asset with similar characteristics like the original.

Now not all forks are intentional, while there is a widely distributed open-sourced codebase, a fork can occur when nodes are not replicating. You should know that forks have a shared history as the record of transactions on the chains is identical before the split.

So there are two programming forks; hard and soft forks. We will begin with the former and move gradually to the latter.

Hard forks

The hard fork is a change made to the protocol that makes the older versions invalid. When older versions continue to operate, they usually end up with different protocols and with different data than newer versions; this can be very confusing and lead to errors in the process.

However, with Bitcoin, a hard fork would be needed to change defining parameters like the block size and the difficulty of getting cryptographic puzzle will need to be solved. The limits to additional information can be added etc. now a change to any of the rules will lead to the acceptance of blocks by the new protocol but rejected by the older one, and this could lead to severe problems, sometimes it could lead to a loss of funds.

So, if the block size limit was increased from 2MB to 5MB, a 3MB block would be accepted by nodes that are running the new version but will not be received by nodes running the older version. So, if a 3MB block is validated by a node that is updated and then placed on the blockchain and the next block is validated and by an operating node, it will add to its block but will detect that the latest block is not valid.

So immediately you've got two blockchains; one that has an older version block and another with the newer version blocks. The chain that grows faster than the other will be determined by the node that has the next blocks validated. The hard fork is generally messy and also risky, so it is possible for bitcoins used on a new block to be spent again on an old block.

The solution to the messy situation with hard fork is for one section to be abandoned for the other, and this means that miners will lose out, the transactions will be lost as well or all the nodes will have to switch to the new version all at the same time (this is so difficult to achieve because we are dealing with a decentralized system)

Soft Fork

The brighter side of this fork is this; it can work with older versions.

So, if a protocol is changed a tightens the rules or adds a function that doesn't affect the structure, the blocks will be accepted by the old version nodes. With Bitcoin, old-version miners will see that their blocks were rejected and then would upgrade. As miners upgrade, the chain with new blocks will become the longest and take over the older blocks.

The system will correct itself, new versions will be accepted, and the latest version becomes the winner. With soft forks, there are no risks attached unlike the hard forks because merchants and users who operate old nodes will read both new and old blocks. If a community wants to reduce the block size to 0.5MB from a limit of 1MB, the new versions will reject the 1MB blocks.

Bitcoins didn't have a block size limit before, but through soft fork the introduction of the 1MB limit became possible. So with forks, you can tell that the soft fork carries way fewer burdens and risks, unlike the hard fork.

The lesson on forks is so valuable because if these systems are not balanced, there will be issues with transactions that are carried out using cryptocurrencies. Remember that the goal of this book is to ensure that you are making the best investment decisions from an advanced level. This means that you will get to know more and do more with knowledge gained.

Have you ever heard about the tokenisation of assets? If you have, you are about to update your knowledge and if you haven't, now is the time to discover more about how cryptocurrency assets are managed.

18

CHAPTER FOUR

Tokenization of assets

Decentralized blockchain networks make numerous investment opportunities for people possible. As it is with the Bitcoin, there is a significant change with the financial scope as such it is possible for the tokenization of assets to make investing in the real world more accessible.

With the tokenization of assets, assets can be divided into smaller units thus ensuring their liquidity and getting other participants to join in. In this chapter, we are going to learn why the tokenization of asset is such a big deal now, why it is the hopeful blockchain application as well as the challenges and chances it presents to investors.

Asset tokenization makes it possible to change the rights of an asset's economic value into a digital token. This process makes it easy to move real-world assets into a blockchain. The tokens can be stored and managed on a blockchain network.

Tokenization has an immense effect on the trading and investment of tokens thus promising transparency, data integrity and increased exchange potential. You can star trading in cryptocurrency fashion through the tokenization of assets. So how does tokenization work?

Asset tokenization progresses naturally with investable funds, here's an example of how this works;

If you are a real estate agent and a property belonging to you is valued at $100,000 you can represent the value regarding tokens using asset tokenization. So if one token is $20, then each token is 0,01% of the shares of your asset. For you to tokenize an asset, it must be evaluated and then an audit should be carried out.

After the evaluation, the tokens are given to the investors. If an individual wants to diversify his/her investment portfolio by adding real estate they can achieve that by buying your tokens on the blockchain. If the property increases in value, it will be represented in tokenized assets as there will be a significant increase in the value of the token as well.

The owners of the tokens will sell at a higher value as well thus increasing the returns on the investment. Are there benefits of assets tokenization? Read on to find out.

The benefits of tokenization

1. They are immutable

When a token is bought, its ownership cannot be erased.

2. Divisibility

There is the promise of liquidity which can increase in value from trade thus eliminating the need for minimum investments.

3. Transparency

While the transfer of ownership is going on, tokens eliminate the measure of information present.

4. The feature of being accessible

You will be able to access tokens from anywhere in the world using a smartphone app.

5. It's cost-effective

With tokens, there is no need for intermediaries, and this also limits the accessibility to investments.

What does asset tokenization mean for a software development perspective? There is the need for a distributed ledger infrastructure for asset tokenization to be developed.

- Firstly, you will need a protocol that consists of a chain of smart contracts to make payments and transfer of legal rights of assets.
- Wallets to store the tokens are also required
- A trading platform that will aid the entire mechanism is a necessary factor.

Different types of tokens can be used for this purpose, and there is a need for different tokens. So below, we will consider two types of tokens.

Types of tokens

1. Utility tokens

This token gives the user access to a product or service; these tokens are used to operate inside a closed blockchain ecosystem and not created as investments. Examples of such investments include; Filecoin and Sia.

2. Security tokens

Security tokens mean ownership of an asset; it can also be used as an economic unit for operations that are on the blockchain and investors can get a profit from them. Examples of such tokens include; Securrency, Securitize and Swarm.

Is real-world asset a game-changer in the world?

Sometimes the facts that ownership of real-world assets on a blockchain can change the way assets are managed. Significant investments like gold, arts and real estate are meant for a few people, but with new means of raising capital through blockchain technology, there will be changes that imply the real world. The implications will be;

1. No middlemen

Trade can be completed without third-parties, think about it for a moment. All the money spent on third-parties can be saved, and the process can be inexpensive and very useful.

2. Improved liquidity of tangible assets

Blockchain tokens can make the introduction of fractional ownership possible, so you get to own part of the assets.

3. Low investment risks

Lower investment risks happen because the investment portfolio becomes diverse as a result of holding a lot of varying assets.

4. Absent of territorial barriers

You can invest from anywhere in the world without leaving the country. Regardless of where you are spending from, you gain access to the same level of speed, security and ease of transfer that is offered by the blockchain network.

There is a new category of cryptocurrency financial product as a result of tokenisation. Assets can be moved to the blockchain, and they include stocks, gold, real estate etc. You should tokenise a precious asset that only a few people can afford, and you can become a trader who is willing to diversify assets that have minimal investment risks.

We have just completed the chapter on tokenisation, and I believe you have learnt a whole lot on how it works. Knowledge gained in this chapter will be very crucial in helping you understand the concepts in the next section.

Regulation is such a big deal when it comes to cryptocurrency; we cannot complete our series on digital currencies without talking about regulations so get ready to learn about ICOs and STOs in the next chapter.

GEORGE SAMARIS

CHAPTER FIVE

Regulations; STOs or ICOs

STOs and ICOs are essential tools in the world of cryptocurrency used in raising funds. While ICO is an acronym for Initial Coin Offering, STO means Security Token Offering. In this chapter, we will learn all about these fundraising tools and how you can utilise them as you invest in cryptocurrencies.

ICOs

An ICO is quite like a crowdfunding event because it is all about how money can be raised for a new project that uses the blockchain technology. With crowdfunding, investors do not have access to the liquidity, and this is the significant difference between it and an ICO.

The individuals who purchase virtual currencies through an ICO can use the coins with a product or attain liquidity by selling their virtual currencies on digital asset trading platforms such as Bittrex.

ICO is likened to the IPO acronym that means Initial Public Offering where companies raise capital through the process of allocating shares to participants. But ICOs are not as regulated as IPOs because with ICOs the focus is on the distribution of tokens and with ICOs the offer to own digital asset is presented on the table. The issue of it been unregulated affects a lot of dreams and aspirations that investors have, and this is one reason STOs are beginning to take the lead (we will learn more about this shortly).

Investors must be mindful of the ICOs they get involved with because so many fraudulent platforms now flaunt ICOs and when unsuspecting individuals get involved, they lose money for good. So, it is always advised that before you invest in any ICO, you should carry out a background check that enables you to get a glimpse into what the company has done in the past and how successful previous ICOs were.

With cryptocurrencies, one must be very mindful of how coins are used. Although ICOs offer a viable investment option, it doesn't hurt much for you to carry out due diligence on the ICO before dropping a coin. Also not all ICOs are successful so when you invest, expect the best while preparing for the worse.

STOs

Security Token Offering ensures the creation of tokens whose value depends on its real-world asset, revenue or existing security stream. The tokens are securities and must follow through with the Security and Exchange Commission. This creates the requirements for token purchasers and gives more time for additional cost for companies who conduct security token offerings to comply with regulations.

One of the first companies that made the notion of STO famous is Polymath, but since their token generation event, ICOs have maintained the lead as the primary fundraising platform. Haven raised billions of dollars in the past ICOs remain a common option in crypto fundraising.

However, ICOs are beginning to slow down regarding popularity, and this is because it is mostly unregulated. Investors want to know that their investments are safe and they need the assurances that security brings.

So with companies like Polymath, they have introduced security token standards like the "ST-20" although the complete adoption of these standards is not entirely mainstream yet. Funding is a make or mar situation for any potential success with blockchain start-ups.

So, if ICOs are banned (because a lack of regulation doesn't work anymore), STOs will most likely become the lifeline of the industry. With STOs it is required that companies follow a registration process, and this will dissuade fraudulent individuals from wanting to carry out nefarious activities that affect investors.

However, the fact that only accredited investors in the United States would participate in purchasing the STOs would reduce the number of potential purchasers who might be interested in the tokens.

So back to the issue of regulation we are faced with, ICOs are not regulated, and that is a huge problem for investors, but STOs proffer a solution to the problem thus making it easier for investors to have options when considering raising funds for their companies using digital currencies. The issue of regulation will always be an issue; so long people invest with cryptocurrencies, they will still have to be mindful of how they use funds.

The fundraising tools are here to stay and while STOs are growing into becoming a healthy alternative for ICOs both tools help players in the industry in developing options on how they can utilise their coins. Every crypto enthusiast will want to learn more about the platforms that are available for use with their currencies.

We will not be talking about fundraising platforms if we don't deal with a significant aspect of cryptocurrencies that make it all possible. I am talking about the blockchain technology. In the next chapter, you will learn more about the blockchain technologies of various coins and how their unique features will make the process of investing easy for you.

CHAPTER SIX

Blockchain technologies

Numerous blockchain technologies are utilised when buying, selling or investing in cryptocurrencies. Generally, a lot of crypto users only get information on the Bitcoin blockchain well, in this chapter, we are going to consider the blockchain technologies of other cryptocurrencies, their uses and unique appeal.

At the end of this chapter, it is expected that the knowledge gained will become instrumental in helping you make better purchasing and investment choices with crypto coins.

Numerous Blockchain technologies

1. Bitcoin blockchain

This is probably the most popular blockchain known to users. The blockchain consist of blocks strung together sand for the new block to be added; some things must happen;

- There must be a transaction
- The transaction must be verified with the public records
- The deal must be stored in a block
- The block must be given a hash

When the new block is added to the blockchain, it becomes available publicly for everyone to sees. The blockchain is very secure, but once details of a bitcoin transaction are attached to the chain, it cannot be altered.

Over the years some people still mix up the significant concepts of Bitcoin and Blockchain, and the clarification process must continue for us to gain a better understanding. While the blockchain technology was first outlined in 1991, the Bitcoin wasn't launched until 2009.

Now the Bitcoin protocol is on the blockchain. So, the people all over the world who have Bitcoins but need a platform to spend it through need the blockchain to make that happen. When a person pays for an item using the Bitcoin, computers on the network verify the transaction.

Just put the Bitcoin the currency used that provides the data the blockchain operates with. If you are keen on investing with the Bitcoin, knowledge of Blockchain technology is crucial.

2. Ethereum blockchain

If you want to build unstoppable applications, then you probably need the Ethereum blockchain. This is a decentralized platform that operates on smart contracts without the possibility of experiencing a downtime.

The blockchain also gives you access to the Ethereum wallet that makes it possible for you to hold and secure ether with other crypto assets that are built on Ethereum.

You can also design and issue your won cryptocurrency, and the tokens will be of standard use that will be compatible with other wallets.

Ethereum makes it possible for you to build a tradeable token with fixed supply, a central bank that can issue money and a puzzle-based cryptocurrency. More importantly, if you have an idea that you want to develop on Ethereum and you need funding, you can kickstart the project through an Ethereum crowd sale.

3. Syscoin Blockchain

Syscoin is a blockchain protocol. It has advanced features that make it possible for you to build high-speed, secure and low-cost applications without glitches. With Syscoin, the concept of the blockchain is taken beyond just a currency as the platform provides a simple and accessible open-sourced development platform that embraces endless possibilities.

With the Syscoin blockchain, you can create and implement decentralised applications that are customizable with the Syscoin Assets. Distributed apps can receive a significant boost using its unique Z-Dag that can send TBA transactions per second while still being distributed and secure.

Syscoin gives a more technological edge to the blockchain technology as you can identify yourself using the web 3.0 that has an optional personal identification mechanism.

Want to build a decentralized marketplace?

Syscoin blockchain also helps you develop your marketplace using the embedded features such as Offers, Certificates, Escrow and Currency Pegging. You can build a whole lot on the Syscoin platform aside from decentralised markets. From storefronts to analytics view and other interfaces.

You can also create crypto tokens and maintain airtight security while being merged with Bitcoin mining making it easier for users to switch from Bitcoin to Syscoin without an increase in cost.

4. Waves Blockchain

With this blockchain, you will be able to gain access to the platform's ability to store, trade, manage and issue digital assets with ease. As an investor, you will be joining the fastest-growing area of the crypto world where multiple currency wallets are created with verified crypto assets.

You can do a whole lot with this blockchain that ranges from taking advantage of their reliable security, transfer funds from person to person and receives interest on your Waves account balance. You can start mining with ease on the Waves platform and create multiple currency wallets.

5. Ripple Blockchain

Ripple is so exciting because it solves the payments problems the world experiences. With Ripple, you can connect with banks and payment providers through the RippleNet to provide an excellent experience for sending and receiving money globally.

There are four essential features, and unique offers Ripple presents to clients;

- Access
- Speed
- Certainty
- Cost

Running on the most advanced blockchain, RippleNet is scalable and interoperates with different networks while giving customers access to source liquidity using the fastest and most reliable digital asset for payment; the XRP.

A lot of banks and payment providers are creating liquidity for payments with new competitive cross-border payments services for customers. Ripple represents a breath of fresh air for crypto users and investors who want to explore a new world of possibility.

6. NEO blockchain

NEO pride themselves in being the network for a smart economy. It is a non-profit community driven blockchain technology with the digital identity. Founded in 201, NEO was open sourced on GitHub in 2015 and has a vast developer community around the world of which CoZ and NEL are significant contributors.

A lot of NEO community users are active on Reddit, GitHub, Twitter and Discord. This blockchain team have succeeded in creating numerous wallets for various platforms, and they have such a keen perception and idea of what they want to achieve in the future. Developers can participate in their projects and get access to NEO and GAS for development testing while viewing technical documentation.

The feature of versatility that is backed by numerous options is one of the most exciting facts about cryptocurrencies. Now that you know the various blockchains and their unique characteristics, you will be able to know exactly what to do with their coins and how to spread your investment in such a way that you have a robust and diverse portfolio.

Aside from blockchain technology, several other platforms have been created to boost user experience with crypto coins. The next chapter takes a look at these platforms and expresses the distinct features they embody. You will enjoy the next section so head over there now and get started.

CHAPTER SEVEN

What are DApps and DAOs?

We are at the last chapter and I know you can't wait to discover what DApps and DAOs are, let's find out, shall we?

Some technologies are created to aid smooth, user-friendly experiences, DApps and DAOs are examples of such creations. DApp is a smart contract that governs the relationship between sunset of network users while DAO is an organisation with bylaws that are encoded in an original deal and be used by employees.

For us to gain an understanding of how both concepts work, we must consider them individually beginning with DApps.

DApps

This is a distributed application that operates its back-end code on a distributed ledger network. DApp can also be referred to as a decentralised application that stores the code within a smart contract which is then linked to a website or a mobile phone app to provide the all-important user-friendly experience.

DApps can be utilised for some cases; users on the platform can exchange goods and services on a peer-to-peer level and still get to enjoy the privileges of electronic payment. However, DApps are governed by a set of rules, for example, you may need specific tokens that are linked to the protocol for particular actions to be executed. So tokens that are related to this protocol become more valuable, and this leads to an increase in the number of people associated with the app.

Currently, Ethereum is the primary choice for DApps because the token is compatible with the DApps system thus making exchanges easier. There are several examples of DApps that will be helpful for blockchain projects and they include; Augur, Slock.it and Storj.

It has been stipulated that DApps should have their token but the Slock. It projects made it evident that DApps doesn't require its tokens. Now if DApp has its tokens, it might become tough converting it to a native token and vice versa yet numerous benefits come with the having a DApp token.

The benefits of DApp tokens

1. Separation of prices

There will be a separation between the prices of ether and DApps token that are used on the network. The value of the DApps token will also not be linked to that of ether as well. There is caveat though: if the price of the native token drops, that of DApps will most likely drop as well.

2.   An incentive for token alignment

Tokens can serve as an alignment for the incentives that developers get as token holders will always be encouraged to support projects by informing people about their goals.

3.   Micromonetary policies

With the DApp community, the users will benefit from having a governance system across the blockchain network. Token holders will have the voting right that determines fund allocation and the approval of new features. This step will lead to monetary policies that will be of immense benefit to users.

DAOs

DAO was the very first large-scale project that launched on the Ethereum network. The project raised over $160 million in ether through an ICO. At the ICO, contributors sent either to a smart contract on the Ethereum platform and got a similar amount of the DAO token in exchange.

DAOs are similar in the way a company works the only difference is the fact that the rules made are enforced digitally. The DAO intends to improve on its governance by giving anyone with access to the internet the opportunity to get DAO tokens or buy them. The creators also want to be able to set the rules thy vote for.

It is quite difficult to change the DAO or a smart contract; this is advantageous because only one person or entity will be unable to change the rules. It has vast disadvantages; if a person gets a bug in, the developers will be unable to change the code

The issue of security with the DAO came to the fore when the platform was attacked, and millions of dollars were drained out. Observers couldn't do anything about it because the hacker followed the rules they established. Although the Ethereum lead coders revered the transaction, it created an unpleasant experience for users and led to a rift between users.

The goal with the DAO concept is this; the creator believes that cryptocurrencies will be able to power leaderless organisations in the future and with the pattern it is taking now such aspirations will most likely become a viable fixture in the cryptocurrency space in the future.

DAOs pride themselves in not requiring help from anyone; they are an independent platform that can make things happen with the digital coin.

DApps and DAOs are just some of the tools that are created to give users of cryptocurrencies a diverse user experience. They are platforms that also showcase the infinite possibilities that abound with digital currencies. So much can be achieved with crypto-coins, it is all about how much you know and how you utilise what you know.

This brings us to the end of the chapter and this book. It has been a worthwhile experience, but there is one more stop to make before we say our goodbyes. In the concluding section below, there is a special message for you; head over there now and discover what it is about.

CHAPTER EIGHT

Altcoin Ninjas; the path way to winning cryptocurrency trading

The team at Altcoin Ninjas recognize that a lot of people have questions about trading, buying and investing with cryptocurrencies hence they are online 24 hours of the day ready to take your questions and enquiries.

This organization was set up for you, they are functioning and working excellently because of you so what will you rather do? You can take advantage of what they offer by becoming a ninja who always on top with all things crypto coins. There are various ways through which you can engage this organization and this just makes it so exciting. As opposed to just having a number to call and talk on, you can actually join the community online and gain access to multiple resources and top-notch personnel that can bridge the gap between you and all the money you can make with crypto coins.

One of the most striking feature of the Altcoin Ninjas organization is the fact that the group isn't just focused on the ways to sell and trade crypto coins. Oh, there is so much more to what they can do for you and one of the numerous services they offer is the sale of unique and effective tools that will aid your trading experience. You will be able to trade in style and comfort with the myriad of tools, materials and equipment offered on the site. Now you can say "goodbye" to the days of trading in discomfort and not knowing the right tools to purchase.

From classy and comfortable chairs to monitors, trading tools, mining equipment and a host of other merchandise. The Altcoin Ninja is your one stop site for information and inventory how cool is that? There is so much more you can enjoy with this group and that includes buying Bitcoin at a 5-8 discount rate than you can find on exchanges, you will be certain of buying real Bitcoins without stress and even getting them at a discounted rate. No scam stories and no delays. You do have the option to become a Samurai or a Sensai; more information on this is on the site. Visit www.altninjas.com and get ready to burst into the world of possibilities with crypto coins.

The world has embraced the concept of social media more than ever before. Now people connect with one another all over the world via social media and who says you cannot do the same with crypto coins? Altcoin Ninjas is active on so many social media platforms; Facebook, Twitter, Instagram, LinkedIn and Pinterest. You can also watch enlightening videos and inspiring content that propels you to make better decisions via YouTube. When you subscribe, you join a movement of people who are passionate about making a difference in their finances with cryptocurrencies and knowing how to go about it the right way.

Altcoin Ninjas organization is more than a site, I can tell you that it is a community that thrives on lifting one another up. There are ninja benefits you enjoy as a member, you just sign up and enter the arena of good vibes and great investment opportunities. Leave the job of carrying out research on ICOs to the Altcoin Ninjas organization, you will also get to know the ICOs they will be investing in thus creating a clear path for you to follow. If you still like there are more questions and concerns bothering you then take a break from chatting with reps and speak directly with the CEO, oh wow! You see, Altcoin Ninjas is strategically positioned to help you become the best version of yourself and also help you get ahead with your cryptocurrency journey.

The reason there is panic within some people with respect to cryptocurrencies is because they have heard of how others make mistakes with their cryptos. Some people who have decided not to invest in crypto coins make their decision based on a lack of understanding of key concepts. However, all of these can be laid to rest when you have a solid team backing you up and providing you with the best services. Altcoin Ninjas was founded on the principle of making life generally easier for its subscribers. We know that money affects the quality of life people live; good money decisions means living well and enjoying life. So, we are dedicated to helping individuals take advantage of the good opportunities crypto coins offer to make their lives better than it is now.

52

Conclusion

What a journey it has been!

Cryptocurrencies are very versatile, and if you want to succeed as an investor, you must be keen on getting all aspects of digital coins that will set you ahead of everyone else.

When we started, we considered the relationship between cryptocurrencies through the years; past, present and future. I hope that the first chapter gave some insight into the evolution of cryptocurrencies and the strategies you can employ in gaining more value for your investment in the future.

Blockchain evaluation, hard and soft forks and the tokenisation of assets are factors you should consider when investing in cryptocurrencies. ICOs, blockchains and dApps all contribute to making the process seamless for you.

The special message I have for you in this section is all about the power of continuous growth. When I wrote the first crypto book for beginners I worked with the data I had then, and everything in that book is different from what we compiled in the second book. Here we are with the third book, and there is a whole different set of knowledge on how to use cryptocurrencies.

If there will be a fourth book, we will have a different approach(s) altogether. So that means you must be able to keep up with novel information on how the world of digital currencies works. Be committed to continuous growth as an individual by seeking out knowledge, reading more and getting exact information needed for the future.

Continuous growth entails filling up the knowledge gap, it is a process that never ends but has exceeding rewards. An investor who is hands-on with getting information will always perform better than the one who is complacent about gaining knowledge. You must always set yourself on course to discover new ideas that make your investment process seamless.

The difference between an investor who excels with cryptocurrencies and the one who doesn't is knowledge. While the former is equipped with the right kind of information, the latter doesn't do anything to seek more knowledge. Never become comfortable with what you know; there is always something better, and it is your responsibility to discover it. Be proactive and deliberate about seeking knowledge.

You have been such a right spot, thank you for sticking it out with me from the beginning to the end. The impact of this book will go a long way in helping you establish stronger ties with your investment portfolio such that every dollar used in digital currency investment will yield results for you.

Another way of ensuring continuous growth is by sharing the details of this book with others in your circle (friends and family). You could set up a crypto book club where you get to share ideas with other investors on how to move forward with investments. Go back to the chapters again after reading and carefully strategize on how to use the steps provided to boost your investments

Thank you for reading.
Best wishes.